THE HEALING COIN

Marion Parrish Hall

DeVorss & Company
Box 550
Marina del Rey, California 90294–0550

Contents

Foreword

Reverend Marion Parrish Hall has done something quite remarkable: written a book on healing which is inspirational, motivational, entertaining, original AND highly practical. As she says in her first chapter, "You can be very spiritual, yet fail to use the mental coin and as a result, continue to suffer." Rev. Hall then proceeds very effectively to explain the nature of healing and the nature of man and how the two can—and should—work in harmony.

I imagine that many interested in spiritual development and all its possibilities are somewhat bored with the many books and tapes relating to spiritual healing that merely "lecture." Rev. Hall's book not only elucidates principles but gives methods for effectively practicing the great laws of mind as they relate to healing. To my way of thinking, her section on Desire, the first requirement for healing, is a small masterpiece and should be read by all. There are many other fascinating chapters and sections of this book; but if none were there, the chapter on Desire would be worth whatever the price of the book.

Rev. Hall writes from her own experience and her own considerable education in the field of "mind science." She has been a most outstanding student in the field; and she has experienced in her life tremendous healing. She knows "whereof she speaks."

I consider it a privilege to recommend this book to all and I sincerely hope that it reaches a very wide audience (whatever her audience, it will be an enthusiastic one.)

Jack H. Holland, Ph.D., D.D.

Jack H. Holland is the author of *Man's Victorious Spirit, Your Freedom to Be, An Outline of Purchasing Management, Love: The Scientific Evidence, The Healing Image and the Perfect Revolution, Divine Energy, Patience: An Aspect of Healing,* and *The "Well" and the "Will."*

Introduction

It is often said that you cannot give away that which you do not have. The methods for healing offered in these pages have been proven to work in my own living laboratory. There were many experiments made, all of which did not work, before I realized that I had to dump out all my old formulas and get to work dissolving ideas and beliefs which caused the pain and sickness that were ruling my life. I can honestly give you these healing formulas because of "squatter's rights." They worked for me and they can work for you. They will work for you to the degree that you work them.

Some of the methods suggested here may appear to be designed for fun and fantasy. There is no reason you should not enjoy your mission of participating in your own healing. Every method has one common purpose, and that is to uproot old ideas and beliefs that have provided you with their correspondent sickness and pain. The best place to begin is right where you are in life. Transformation can begin no other place. Paul said, "Be ye transformed by the renewing of your mind." Every suggestion is for correction of perception, so be prepared to let go of some of the viewpoints which have caused you to see the world and those in your life in a particular way.

You will find the mental and spiritual coins for this transformation herein.

NEW VISTAS

How vast Thy seas and skies,
How high Thy unfolded Infinity,
How wondrous before my eyes,
The precious brush strokes
Of Divinity.

Sweet Spirit, Thy tender strength
Embraces me with such loving care,
Guiding my feet the breadth and length,
Leaving me never.
Thou art always there.

Was there a day I knew you not?
A morn when I forgot your Beloved Name?
Though, once a thief who stole from self,
I have at last found Truth,
And am free from pain.

Now give me more days to declare,
And give me new vistas for sight,
And give me the right to share
Thy handiwork,
This moment of my life.

—Marion Parrish Hall

CHAPTER 1

The Healing Coin

Every man must pay the price for that which he receives and that price is paid in mental and spiritual coin.

—Ernest Holmes, THE SCIENCE OF MIND

THE LAW OF mental and spiritual payment is enforced on everyone. The payment for the good you desire must be rendered in advance. There is no way that law can be changed. It is necessary to pay in both mental and spiritual coin. This law cannot be set aside to accommodate any person or any thing.

You can be very spiritual, yet fail to use the mental coin and as a result, continue to suffer. You can pay the mental coin but be delinquent in spiritual payment and continue to bring pain and suffering into your life. How, then, are you to manifest the mental and spiritual coin to pay for wellbeing? You have tried many suggestions but have experienced much failure.

Are you ready to follow some very simple, almost childlike mental and spiritual exercises to change beliefs which have caused pain and suffering, beliefs of a lifetime? If so, I will share with you some of the exercises I learned to use to go from sickness and pain to wellness. I am still using them today.

PAYMENT DAY

There was no way the car could avoid us that November morning in 1980 as it shot through the stop signal to slam into the passenger side of the car where I sat. In those few fragments of a moment, my life flashed before me and a decision established, "I don't want to die. I have too much to do." Then came the crash with all its grinding sounds.

I did, indeed, have much work to do. I was the founding minister of a small church of Religious Science in Yucaipa, California, that was only three months old.

The strength of my ministry was teaching the Principles of healing and for a very good reason. It was because of a remarkable healing that I first began earnestly to study Science of Mind and finally to become a minister. Just twenty-four hours before the accident, my husband, John, had taken a Sunday away from his own pulpit, ninety miles away, to join me in my church for a joint message with questions and answers about healing. Following the collision, I was to have the opportunity to prove, once again, that the Spiritual and mental Principle works.

While my body was being crushed under the impact and even through the terrible pain which followed, I did not lose consciousness. In the grinding sounds of the crash, I heard a snap in my back. My legs and hips folded in a peculiar fashion upon impact. I struggled for breath. I knew my chest was in trouble because of the slam of metal that had hammered into it with the one violent blow.

Pain as I had never experienced took over my body and attempted to possess my mind. But, somehow I kept my clarity. I knew there was only one help for me, and I needed it now. Recognition of the One Presence in my broken bones and crushed body allowed me to retain a higher consciousness throughout the physical experience. My inner life was not touched.

The calmness that followed was the result of my holding to this Spiritual Lifeline. This knowledge of the Presence was the only Reality that could help me that bleak day. From the very moment of impact, I affirmed the Presence, "God is here," "God is in my body" and other statements of recognition of Omnipresence.

The paramedics tried to pull away the door which imprisoned me, but to no avail. I continued to affirm God in whispers. Finally, after removing my husband, who had broken ribs and a fractured foot, they dragged my body across the seat and out the door on the driver's side. I continued to recognize my Higher Power. Had I not done this, I might have lost consciousness at this point.

In the emergency room at the hospital in Hemet, California, I was aware that the greatest pain in this symphony of discord was located in my back. My husband, John, was on the table near me, with a curtain drawn between us. I called out to him, only able to say, "John, treat . . . my back!" Spiritual treatment, as it is known to New Thought, is affirmative prayer. John treated for my perfect back.

Most remarkable was the fact that my back never gave me pain throughout my recovery period, although evidence of a compound fracture of a lower back vertebra was shown to me a year later by my chiropractor. Just after the X-rays were made, the day of the injury, one of my medical team told me of my injuries and mentioned that the fracture in the back would have to heal itself; there was nothing they could do about it. I dismissed it after that, because it did not pain me.

The Law of Cause and Effect certainly was working for me in a dramatic way. The causes that manifest as one effect can be many. No doubt causes of fear of being hit, mistakes I had even forgotten, and even the desire to know more about this Healing Power I taught were responsible for the incident that November day. Perhaps deep within me the desire to share this knowledge with many others required this traumatic happening to make it possible to write this book. But to advance in our Spiritual awareness, it is not important to be overly concerned with past causes. We work to have a greater recognition of God. As we come into alignment with our Higher Power, new causes take the place of the old. These bring reflective experiences, which we understand as good. It is also possible to find good in a painful experience, but that requires correction of perception. And that is what this book is all about.

THE VALUE OF RECOGNITION

It was not conscious reasoning that brought me to the recognition of the Divine Presence that Monday morning, but the same instinct that causes a small child to reach out to a parent for comfort and a feeling of safety when he is hurt.

Even as I was pried from the wreckage, I voiced affirmations of that Presence. I repeated them constantly during the hours and days to come, as though it was a means of survival. Now, I know that it was just that. The recognition of Spirit is the greatest technique for healing and changing conditions.

The week that followed, I lived in a body of broken bones and internal injuries, struggling for each breath. Vital signs were monitored to indicate when it was advisable to perform surgery. I slept very little and was conscious throughout the experience. My conscious contact with that Higher Power was my life-line to sanity. I refused pain medication most of the time. This was not due to bravery on my part but to the gut-feeling that this recognition of the Higher Power was the only permanent help I was going to get.

THE GIFT

Remarkable things began to happen. I found That Presence manifesting in everyone in my physical and thought atmosphere as well as my ability to stay calm during intense pain. It was the beginning of the "Gift." Busy ministers offered their services and spoke in the pulpit of my new church. Friends and total strangers came in great numbers to share their love and encouragement, and inspiring cards and letters told me that many were praying for me. One nurse came by each day after her shift just to talk with me and to bring small gifts. Loving in-laws and ministers in the area were a constant comfort.

I was finding the "Gift" in everything and in everyone. I was in a state of awareness which was only accountable to my constant seeking The Presence. This I share with you who suffer pain, because it is a "Gift" you can seek and find when you remain in a state of recognition of the Presence of God. It is easy to come to believe in the power of pain when your body is experiencing it. A shift in consciousness to recognize the power of that Something Greater brings about a change that I was experiencing. The "Gift" was to continue.

VERDICT, NOT REALITY

Surgery required four and a half hours; and during my two weeks in the hospital, eight units of blood were used. It was only after surgery that I was able to actually sleep, one week following the accident.

When a member of my surgical team saw me later, he was very proud of work well done, for the results had exceeded all expectations. He explained the nature of the injury and the repair that had been done. Then in a quiet voice, he said, "You will probably never walk again." After a week of constantly experiencing a higher awareness than I had ever known, I knew that with this Higher Help the doctor's verdict had no power to prevent me from experiencing life to the fullest. I needed to walk to do this. I wanted to walk, and I would walk.

I informed the doctor I would walk again. He gave me a sad little smile and ignored my comment. He advised me that there would always be the presence of pain. There was much metal in my limbs and hip; and I did live with pain for several months, but that too was not a permanent condition. Had I accepted the belief in disability and pain, I would have given them support. I denied the verdict.

ACTION AND SEEING AHEAD

To avoid using energy to resist pain, I chose to get busy on a program of helping myself to a healing. A 'victory diary' was my special project. I recorded at least one victory each day. Victory was refusing pain medicine, and victory was straightening my bedside table. My 'victory diary' became a source of secret pride. This was action, and I knew if I started doing things, I would continue doing until someday I would walk again. Each victory recorded encouraged me to do more.

I had a lot of time to use my creative mind, and I did. I visualized myself walking. I mentally put down my foot, being careful (in mind, of course) to use all the muscles in the way I had always used them to walk. I saw myself walking smoothly, without limping. I visualized waking from a night of painless sleep. I used my creative imagination to influence my belief in a total healing.

I remembered the words of Jesus, "It is done unto you as you believe." I did not allow myself the luxury of self-pity. I was not being heroic, but I knew that self-pity would only prolong the problem and would not produce a healing. I understood the Principle and how It worked, and I wanted to return to my ministry and to walk again.

SIGNS OF HEALING

Four days after my doctor had given his verdict, he stood at the foot of my bed, reading my chart and murmuring, "It's amazing!" I heard him repeat this two more times.

I asked, "Are you amazed at my recovery?" He answered, "I would never have thought this possible or that I could release you this early, but you can go home Sunday." This was one week after surgery.

WHERE SHALL I TURN?

After I returned to Yucaipa, my husband and I discovered an unexpected problem. There was no live-in help available. John was on crutches, but he attended to my needs even with his temporary handicap. He was the minister of the Magnolia Park Church in Burbank, California, where we also maintained a residence. For nearly a year we had commuted from one home to the other, yet managing to serve our respective churches. This resulted in a strain on our home life but not on our relationship. Our love spanned the miles.

John's injuries and my needs had kept him away from his ministry for four weeks. Two weeks after I returned home, he was well enough to serve in his church. I insisted he return to Burbank, for the congregation had missed his leadership. He protested but finally left, reluctantly. Someone was to come to help me within the hour.

John left in good faith, but the nurse did not arrive. I was almost totally helpless. I could not refill my water glass, go to the bathroom, go to the kitchen for food, or reach the thermostat to regulate the heat. There was an hour or so where I had to rise above what appeared to be and use my faith. Could the Spirit that had been my help and comforter thus far fill these needs now? I remembered the promise in the Psalms, "Yea, though I walk through the valley of the shadow of death, I will fear no evil for Thou art with me."

HELP FROM A STRANGER

John had left the door unlocked for a nurse who didn't come, but someone else did come. It was Cathy McCune, a neighbor, whom I had never met before the accident. She came in response to a 'feeling' that I might need help. She might have been an angel, for that is how she seemed to be, arriving at such a time in my need. Cathy was a retired nurse. She immediately performed all the wonderful things an experienced nurse knows to do. She prepared my evening meal and informed me that she would come again in the morning.

I couldn't have visualized a better angel than my neighbor Cathy proved to be. Cathy refused any payment for the fine care she gave to me during this period of my recovery. She told me the story of a time following a tragic accident when she received the loving care of her neighbors. She insisted she was only returning to the Universe the gift she had once received. In the months to come, Cathy was always there when I needed her.

My husband John was always faithful to support me in my healing practices, always believing as I did that I would walk again. He was in Yucaipa each week from Wednesday afternoon through Saturday afternoon; then I would send him off to Burbank for his Sunday service.

THE LIMITLESS SEA OF RECEPTIVITY

Ernest Holmes told us that one who could throw himself into the Limitless Sea of Receptivity, having cut loose from all apparent moorings, would always receive the greatest reward. During the months ahead, I seemed to be doing just that. I was testing those very waters of receptivity and finding unusual rewards. There were nights when I was alone with only the knowledge that there was a loving Presence to care for me, an unseen Keeper to quiet my fears. I had to trust, and I found I could trust. Without trust in God's loving care, I would not have managed the strength or balance to move from my bed to a wheelchair. I was weak in body, and such a move, alone, was a great challenge. It was obvious if I lost my balance or my strength failed me, I would fall and lie on the floor until someone came and found me.

My doors remained unlocked when I was alone, but I never feared trouble entering my door. This desire to trust was the need fulfilled. I am thankful today for the experience that taught me the real meaning of trust. It was in this trust that I realized that I could return to my pulpit to give my message, even standing on one leg. So, I talked to God a lot, putting myself in the care of my Higher Power, sometimes on a minute-to-minute basis.

VICTORIES

Although John was very supportive, he didn't always understand when I insisted on doing things which he could easily do for me when he was at home. I had learned to wheel myself into the kitchen, cook simple things, and even wash dishes from my wheelchair. I realized that just enjoying his help could also become a 'benefit.' I didn't want any benefits to make my condition so comfortable that I would settle for this way of life permanently. I have seen those who made that kind of settlement, and the cost of such benefits is too high. Besides, I was still recording in my victory diary, and every handicap overcome went into my diary. Little by little, I was correcting my perceptions of limitation. I had a price to pay for my healing, and it was paid in trust and action. Ernest Holmes reminded us that there was a price to pay for the good life, and that was "mental and spiritual coin." I added a little "physical coin" to that.

In the hospital I had set a goal to return to my pulpit on December 14. There was little encouragement for this decision. My doctor told mc that returning to my duties of the ministry was out of the question for as much as a year. But what could you expect from a rebel who has been told this? I refused to accept the verdict, of course.

December 13 my son Marc and his wife Barbara arrived unexpectedly from Texas. The next morning Barbara dressed me, Marc put me in his car with the wheelchair in the trunk, and off we went to church.

In the presence of the largest congregation the young church had ever had, and with my son and daughter-in-law seated before me, I realized I was being showered with blessings by my Higher Power.

I spoke on the one thing I had experienced, "The Gift in Your Problem." It was one of the happiest days of my life and another victory. From then on I continued to serve in my pulpit.

TAKE UP THY BED AND WALK

Six and a half months after the accident, I walked. I did so without limping, just as I had visualized. The pain the doctor had warned me as being permanent had moved and was gone. Today my husband no longer needs to drive ninety miles to be with me. He is the minister of a church only twelve miles from home, and he is with me under one roof in Yucaipa.

STAY ON COURSE

The methods I used to heal my body and at the same time improve the quality of my life, I give to you. The only price you have to pay for your healing is paid by mental and spiritual coin, by correcting perceptions of limitation, and in learning to trust a Power Greater than you are. By now you know what that Power is. You can use these steps given to participate in your own healing, regardless of your problem, if you are willing to change your course and stay on it.

MIND

Mind is the Master-Power
That molds and makes,
And man is Mind,
And everywhere he takes
The tool of thought,
And shaping what he wills,
Brings forth a thousand joys,
A thousand ills.
He thinks in secret
And it comes to pass:
Environment is but
His looking-glass.

—James Allen, *As a Man Thinketh*

CHAPTER 2

The Mind That Can Heal

. . . Pride, leading to self-justification and always spurred by conscious or unconscious fears, is the basic breeder of most difficulties, the chief block to true progress.

—From *Twelve Steps and Twelve Traditions*
Alcoholics Anonymous World Services, Inc.

THE COIN FOR FOUNDATION REPAIR

OFTEN IN NEW THOUGHT PHILOSOPHY there is a tendency to deny the rock in the shoe. You might think, "If I don't see it, the rock is not there." But the rock IS there. Infinite Intelligence through you knows the rock is there as a message and can be removed when you find it and get the message. You must remove it by first facing the problem, then the cause. Only then can you successfully remove the cause.

Ego-made flaws: criticism, guilt, anger, resentment, fear, and unforgiveness must be faced and recognized as the faulty structure in your spiritual foundation. Such recognition takes painful honesty, and it is much more comfortable to pretend it is not there while going about smiling and saying, "But, I always think and say good things about myself and others." This is the pride that goes before the fall.

You actually deceive yourself when you cease to discover things which can be changed to repair this structure. When you continue to declare the emperor's new clothes when the emperor is naked, you are living a lie and have stopped your spiritual progress. (For those who do not know the story of the Emperor's New Clothes: The clever faker of the new clothes claimed to have woven beautiful fabrics from invisible threads and fashioned clothing visible only to the pure in heart. The impure could only see a naked emperor, so the faker declared.)

In Alcoholics Anonymous this lie is exposed when the alcoholic takes the fourth step in the "Twelve suggested steps in Recovery." He searches his mind and life for destructive and ego-centered defects and mistakes. These he can no longer deny. He makes a list of them, no matter how painful they are to face. This is not at all harmful to his self-esteem because on the other side of the sheet he lists his strengths.

Once his inner thoughts and defects are revealed, he takes one more step in disposing of the lies which have been causing his problems. He shares these character defects with another person, one who understands the purpose of the stripping away process. Now, the alcoholic has discovered the rock in his shoe and is ready to work to remove it.

The most difficult counseling this writer has ever done is with the person who is in pain and trouble but will not expose to light the cracks in his structure which are the basic cause. He firmly attests that the emperor is wearing clothes. He will not bear the pain of recognizing and exposing the weaknesses that cause and contribute to his problem. The real problem, however, is not the effect, but the cause.

Revealing your weakness, exposing your innermost feelings is a giant step in your recovery. This exposure does not make you a lesser person; rather, a far wiser and stronger person, because you are taking the most important step in your own healing. It does not label you as bad or wrong, merely as an evolving person. When you no longer need to learn and evolve from defects because you are perfect, your purpose of evolution can no longer be served by life in the present body.

Out of the defect, the mind creates an effect which carries a message. The message says, "Here is a crack in your foundation. Fix it." The crack, when recognized, is an opportunity for growth.

The defect then becomes a gift. The coin that you pay for it is recognition and repair. Your healing begins.

YOU CAN CHANGE YOUR LIFE

All we need is a key and the decision to swing the door open. There is one key and it is called willingness.

—From *Twelve Steps and Twelve Traditions*
Alcoholics Anonymous World Services, Inc.

You, the beloved creation of God, are given all the attributes of the Divine Nature and allowed to use or misuse them.

GOD'S ATTRIBUTES:

- Life
- Love
- Choice
- Creative Law

You are free to use these attributes, and you use them one way or another at all times.

Creative mind of man produces the idea or belief, and Creative Law acts to manifest experiences that correspond to the idea or belief. Law mirrors all thought back into your life through people, places or things. This is an absolute law. Understanding of the nature of this law dissolves the old idea that it is God's will that you suffer.

The good news is that you can change your life and be healed by the same law that brought forth your pain and sickness. When you change the tendency of thoughts and form new beliefs, circumstances once created by old perceptions begin to change. You *can* change your life and even heal your body.

When you realize you have created all conditions in your life, you will understand that this Law always works and never says "no" to your choices. It is a law just like electricity and gravity. It serves to produce only what you believe to be true. Ernest Holmes stated, "We are surrounded by a Creative Law which receives the direct impress of our thought and acts upon it."

The Creative Law acts upon what you believe, not just what you think you believe. Once your belief is set in the subjective mind, it begins to form a mold for an effect which corresponds with it. If belief is resentment, guilt, anger, lack or sickness, the Creative Law produces a corresponding experience. If belief is in freedom, love, joy, prosperity or wellness, the Law produces accordingly. Everything and everyone needed to bring about the working out of the Law is provided.

The Law makes no judgments; it is not partial. It is just the Divine Operator that functions on the same principle as does the computer. The conscious mind can be taught to accept a new belief that brings about the result you want. You can use the Creative Law for good.

DESIRE

Desire is the first requirement for your healing. You must place your wellness at the top of your priority list and be willing to make the mental and spiritual sacrifices for it.

George W. Meek, who spent ten years studying healing arts of many cultures and persuasions, writes in *Healers and the Healing Process:*

> Healing will seldom start, and it will not be permanent, unless there is a desire on the part of the patient to return to health. The patient cannot be well unless he wants to be well more than he wants to be ill, and once healed, he will not stay well, unless he wants to stay well. Often, of course, the patient is unaware of this.

Frequently, sickness and pain are tolerated until a decision becomes unavoidable. One becomes sick and tired of being sick and tired. It is then that desperation becomes a powerful goad. When one realizes that he is facing an unknown fork in the road and a decision must be made whether to go on as before or to make a change, he then is a likely candidate for healing. Desperation may provide the incentive necessary to put forth the mental energy that makes healing possible. It is this motivated person who will make the sacrifices, learn the disciplines, and be willing to change the patterns of thought which have brought about his condition. He will begin by correcting his perceptions. He has started on a magnificent journey of discovery.

Because of an accident which threatened my lifestyle, I made a conscious decision to be healed and to use whatever disciplines were necessary. You, too, can be healed, or even avoid illness and pain, by following these principles, by paying the mental and spiritual coin.

A commitment is necessary. To start the action (and action is essential to your healing) begin with the first step. It is a mental coin. It is a contract of commitment. You will be actually making this promise to yourself. Remind yourself of it often. This conscious contract for healing is for you alone:

I, ______________________________________
(write your name)
commit my thoughts, energy and efforts to be well. I willingly make healthy changes in my beliefs and attitudes. I release all benefits I have enjoyed, or in some way profited from, because of my problem. I accept my healing.

Now for the techniques for your healing . . .

CHAPTER 3

Techniques For Your Healing

Warning: The following information may be dangerous to the ego. Side effects may be experienced: mental regurgitation, indigestion of ideas, unexplained fear, and sudden resistance or anger.

When taken as directed with open mind and courage, the result will be an 'undoing' which removes obstructions to healing.

SOME OF THE TECHNIQUES for healing are fun, but to experience a wellness that is permanent, certain offenders need to be recognized and removed. Until this is done, there cannot be an attitude of wellness. The offenders are the property of ego.

If you feel threatened by these revealing facts about ego, guess what is being threatened? Every person has created and invested in personal ego; therefore, every person is prepared to defend it. You may fear that once the ego is removed, the real thinking, feeling you will be removed. This is not true. Our greatest lovers of mankind and those who have 'gone the extra mile' for humanity have had no great investment in ego.

> The ego is the part of the mind that believes your existence is defined by separation.
>
> —From *A Course in Miracles*

The fear of death, need for justification, defense, guilt, competition, self-pity, war, and on and on, all are products of ego. Ego is strong in its own defense, because it is struggling to survive. It knows you are greater than itself. You are far greater. You are the Divine Image. You were created in the image and likeness of God; ego was not. God made you, but your own false beliefs made ego.

Now, are you ready to view ego's operation honestly and make some important changes in your life?

FACING YOUR FEAR

> *Fear is the reverse mental attitude of faith and is the result of the lack of faith. Fear brings limitation and lack in its wake and destroys the happiness and possibility of a greater degree of livingness to those who suffer from it.*
>
> —Ernest Holmes, *The Science of Mind*

Fear is a phenomenon in nature because it is common only to thinking and instinctive life. Fear in itself is not an entity and cannot harm or destroy; it is nothing appearing to be something. Fear is the creation of the fearful. It is a motivating emotion because it is given power by the one experiencing it.

The purpose fear serves in primitive or animal life is survival. But man, created in the image and likeness of God, has been given an intelligence, a creative mind, and above all, a spiritual nature which makes fear superfluous. Even with intelligence and creative mind, man can allow fear to control; but when he uses the guidance in his spiritual nature, when he trusts that Nature, which we call God, all his intelligence and his creative mind are put to work for his survival and even more.

Trust is the complete opposite of fear. Trust is not always easy. How can you trust when you are in pain or when the doctor is telling you that your disease is terminal? This is the time when you must throw out all belief in the absoluteness of the pain or disease and step out on the waters of an Absoluteness that is more powerful and more true than circumstances. It is a Power which makes all things possible. If you succeed in this, you have revealed fear for what it is. You have evolved to a far greater spiritual ground than you've ever attained before.

In the 23rd Psalm, we read: ". . . I will fear no evil for Thou art with me . . ." In faith, we release fear, but what if you are in disease and pain and in that state make the transformation into trust in the Power which can heal you? You now recognize that past fears have brought about these problems, and you know that the Law of cause and effect is working. Is there any way to get out of that pattern you have established? The answer is "yes." Your new cause, which can give you the physical and spiritual transformation you want, is to release fear and establish trust. This is the first step, and perhaps the hardest, but you can do it.

Because there is no waste in nature, your problem cannot be wasted. It can be used to bring more of the same experience, or it can be used for you to make that giant leap, an evolution which you would not have made without the painful experience. I would never have changed my life and entered the ministry if I had not been ready and able to surrender fear for faith and trust. I would not have given up my ministry in a small church, in order to reach larger groups of people with a powerful healing message in workshops and books, if I had not been further transformed by faith and been healed after a life-threatening accident in 1980.

We tend, too readily, to welcome the belief of race consciousness that accepts certain diseases as terminal. In every century there has been a so-called "killer disease" that has brought fear to the hearts of millions, because they accepted this race belief.

In Jesus' time the disease was leprosy, and down through the ages there have been many diseases to strike terror to civilization: black plague, tuberculosis, diabetes, heart disease, infantile paralysis. And, as each number-one "killer disease" in turn moved over to make room for a winning candidate, the now number-two disease, in the absence of the energy of fear, began to lose power. Fear that man created for survival's sake has threatened his survival.

Today's greatest supporters of race consciousness of pain and disease are the news media. A new or recurring disease is given energy and acceptance by the fear generated by this wide coverage. We can rise above this influence by denial. This is not closing our minds to facts, but a denial that we are threatened by any outside power.

> The Plague, on its way to the city, passed an old man on the side of the road. "Where are you going?" asked the old man. "I am going to the city to kill a thousand people," Plague answered.
>
> A year later, Plague passed the old man on the road while returning from the city. "You told me that you were going to the city to kill a thousand, but instead you killed ten thousand," the old man said.
>
> "I told you the truth; I killed a thousand people. Fear killed the rest!"
>
> —Anonymous

Remember that it is your own mind that produces fear. Face your fear and recognize it for the impostor it is. Forgive yourself for entertaining it and put your trust in a Power that is real. That is your spiritual and mental coin.

DEALING WITH GUILT

We should also erase the thoughts of yesterday that would rob us of today's happiness.

—Ernest Holmes, *The Science of Mind*

You are not on trial for action, non-action, or false beliefs of the past. You are not guilty. The only time for which you are accountable is this very moment. Since reading the last sentence, you are in a new moment. You are no longer responsible for the past, but you may use the effect of past mistakes to reveal a better way of doing things. You were not created to carry the self-made burdens of yesterday. The Spirit within you is unblemished and beyond wonders. The only blemishes that can be seen are those created by the ego, and they are not real. Memories can be healed when exposed to this truth.

Guilt causes you to feel unworthy. Often the roots of this feeling may be found in the early, impressive years.

Milly understood the Principles of New Thought, and she was an eager student; but her life history was one of pain and sickness. In spite of many demonstrated healings, the pattern of sickness and pain persisted. She came to me first with an ear infection. Within a week after prayer, the problem was gone. This was the beginning of my experience with her very real troubles. There followed a tumor visible on her neck. She responded to prayer treatment with a healing.

In the first three years I knew Milly, there were many healings. Although we rejoiced with each healing, it became apparent that Milly had never been healed of the true cause: the need to be sick and in pain. She, too, realized that there was a message in the pattern. Milly came in for counseling. We talked about forgiveness. It was obvious that she was not carrying any loads of resentment or anger. I asked her, "How do you feel about your own self?" A light came to her eyes. It was an 'Ah ha' light.

Then she told me something about her childhood. She had been an only child and had enjoyed the affection of loving parents; but when she was very young, she first heard her mother make a statement that was to be repeated several times in her life. Her mother, a very beautiful and sophisticated lady, had said, "I never intended to have any children, but Milly was my mistake."

After Milly entered school, her mother became very sick and remained so for many years. How do you suppose Milly could be worthy of her mother's acceptance? She could join her mother in physical misery. She could do nothing about the rejection which she still carried, but she could suffer punishment for being unworthy of being born. Where there is a feeling of guilt, there is a subconscious desire to be punished.

It took some time for Milly to understand that her birth was not a mistake. Her mother was only a channel for God's expression as Milly. Such old belief patterns are not easy to break, but they can be replaced by a new idea of worthiness, by understanding that your true nature is that of God expressed as *you.* Milly was able to change the old idea of being a mistake. She then no longer needed repeated healings. There was nothing left to heal.

You have always done the best you have known how to do. If you had known better, you would have chosen differently. It is true that ego guides falsely, but the wrong path taken in the past can only be traveled again in your painful memories. There is no traveling backwards in time, only in memory. Guilt is an unhealed memory of a false belief or choice.

Examine your feelings about past mistakes, rejections, and failures. If possible, talk it out with a confidant. When you find guilt, begin a prayer program of self-forgiveness. Each day, begin with facing yourself in the mirror and addressing the person you see there with a freeing affirmation, "You are God's expression. You are without guilt." Wouldn't you say the same to a suffering friend?

Self-forgiveness is the answer for a healing of guilt. You have been taught to forgive others. Now, you are asked to forgive yourself. Say to yourself, "I forgive the past, and I accept the gift of a healed memory." This is a releasing affirmation and your redemption from guilt.

JUDGING OTHERS . . . AND YOURSELF

That which you deny existence in your own life you often see in others. Sitting in the seat of judgment of others can temporarily block the pain of examining your own inner world. But, the pain always returns. You draw yourself a little higher on your chart of 'right and wrong,' a mental chart created by your own ego. Ego must justify its ability to judge and has made it convenient to do so by such evaluation. There is no potential for weakness that you do not share with your brother. Judgment of others is the recognition of your own possibilities.

Jesus said, "Judge not that you be not judged." How can anyone be expected to give up this defense mechanism? It is a habit which was created in the early bloom of ego. However, you do not have to go it alone. Spirit will not change your thoughts, but will, upon request, provide a way for you to recognize the Christ in your fellows and also yourself.

Do you want a mental alarm system to remind you when you are thinking amiss? Ask the Father within for this witnessing of your thoughts. Be ready to see others as Divine creations that are experiencing actions and emotions that are necessary for them at this time in their evolution. Excuse yourself from making judgment. Be willing to change. Listen for the alarm system and respond to it.

As you begin to respond to that Divine alarm system and recognize Christ in others, your tendency to judge will begin to lose power. The need to judge will no longer dominate you. When that happens, you will find that you are experiencing the Christ within yourself. Your own stock will go up. You have removed an obstruction to your own healing.

Clara had been under medication to prevent the return of phlebitis for several years. Her problem had been diagnosed as thrombosis. She constantly suffered with lack of circulation in her feet and ankles, which were purple, cold, and almost without feeling. After entering a prayer treatment class, Clara began working in Spiritual Mind Treatment for a healing.

When her physical condition remained the same, I suggested she honestly examine her thoughts and feelings for any mental obstructions that could be restricting this natural flow of life. This she did and later shared with her group that she had long resented a certain woman whom she blamed for her husband's unfaithfulness. Clara explained that seven years ago, because of her own business commitments, she had been absent from home, often leaving her husband alone for days at a time. It was at this time that he had an affair with the woman who once had been a mutual friend of theirs. Later, in remorse, he confessed his unfaithfulness to Clara. Following the confession, Clara began to experience problems with her feet and ankles.

When sharing with the class, Clara decided to pray for the woman she had so long resented. About ten days later, she admitted she no longer resented the other woman. She said she had forgiven both her husband and the other woman; however, her condition remained the same. Apparently, there was still a problem concerning release of the past.

Clara was a good student who really wanted to participate in her own spiritual growth as well as her physical healing. Her continuing problem puzzled her until one day an idea came to her. The one person that she had not released from this traumatic experience was her own self. She still blamed herself for leaving her husband in this vulnerable position. She had simply transferred the guilt from the other woman to herself.

When she understood that by blaming herself she had not released the past at all, she began to pray to see the Christ within herself. Within twenty-four hours, Clara felt a moment of painful tingling in her feet. At first she was alarmed; then she realized that the feeling had returned to her feet and ankles, the restriction of circulation had been removed. She had been limiting the natural flow of blood to these parts by holding back the natural flow of love from herself. Once she forgave herself, her problem was no longer necessary as a means of delivering a message of the inner disorder.

An old American Indian prescription for healing the body includes these mental and spiritual steps: desire to be well, faith, forgiveness, and willingness to change. Forgiveness is a vital ingredient in your own healing.

REMOVING RESENTMENT

All anticipation or memory of discord invites destructive experiences, promotes physical discomfort, and is harmful to relationships. Resentment and hate can prevent your healing.

It is the ego's belief that someone is capable of taking something from you. The ego demands more approval than you are getting. Fear that others can deny you your good, or will not approve or validate you, causes you to react to others with resistance. If there is one you resent or hate, ask yourself what you believe the other is trying to take from you. Does another fail to approve of you? How tolerant are you of those who do not threaten your ego? Recognize the part the ego plays in troubled relationships. Meditate on it with total honesty. Such self-facing can remove many problems involving resentment.

You can find relief from the bitter emotion of hate when you pray for the one resented, if you pray aright. Too often we pray for another with ideas that might resemble this: "I'll forgive the rascal if it kills me." It is better that you pray for your own freedom from discord than to pray for the offender with renewed attention to the offense. Through prayer you can replace the energy of hate with the energy of love. Remember, energy is neutral and may be used to build as well as to destroy.

If you are not ready for the prayer program for release of resentment and hate, try replacing the troubled memory with creative thoughts that are not associated with the person or experience. In this way the discordant thoughts lose their place of importance.

Forgiveness is a self-serving act. It releases pent-up energy of anger and resentment which is harmful to the body and affairs. Can you afford to let unresolved conflicts to do their thing in your body? Of course not!

Forgiveness is not always easy or comfortable to produce; but when you continue to seek a way to forgive, you are insured of finding the way.

Since forgiving is self-serving, giving to the one you seek to forgive is 'other-serving.' What gift can you best give than the good from your own spiritual storehouse? You have heard the adage, "To give is to receive." The belief that to give is to create lack in self, is false. So as you other-serve, you self-serve.

Here is how you can give from your spiritual storehouse: when you think of the person whom you resent, mentally say his name, then say, "I send you my peace and joy." Each time you think of the person, repeat the affirmation gift. Visualize him as peaceful and joyful. Continue this other-serving program until you transcend resentment. You will begin to understand the part your ego has played in the origin of the anger and resentment. You will see the part your peace and joy is playing in your act of forgiveness.

Here are questions to ask yourself about unresolved resentment:

1. Have I carried this resentment long enough?

2. What rewards do I receive from resentment?

3. Whom am I punishing with this resentment?

4. Do I want to be punished? If so, why?

5. Am I ready to release the pains of resentment?

Elizabeth Klumpp, my own practitioner, recommends this affirmation:

> I am mentally, emotionally, and physically free from all false attitudes, concepts, beliefs, ideas of self-rejection, and self-condemnation that I have entertained concerning every person, place, thing, and activity in my life, from the moment I was conceived up to today and eternally. And, those false attitudes are free from me.

The purpose of this affirmation is to replace old destructive ideas with healed thoughts. Whatever means you use, if it takes the energy from discord, you have experienced a healing. Since hate and resentment are energies, a punching bag may be your answer; but remember, transcending the problem is better than beating it to death.

RECOGNIZING ILLNESS "BENEFITS"

The British Health Services conducted a four-year investigation into the medical history of Stewart McIlroy, who had been admitted to sixty-eight different hospitals on at least two-hundred and seven occasions. McIlroy changed his name twenty-two times and became a master of medical jargon to describe his symptoms. His body was a road map of surgical scars. The estimated cost was stated to be as high as $1,000,000, all paid for by the British Health Services.

It is hard to imagine the benefits this man received from his experience; yet such self-torture, to a lesser degree, is not uncommon.

The benefits of sickness and pain can be the following: power over spouse or family, sympathy, attention for you who have always felt deprived, an acceptable excuse to avoid responsibility, and self-pity. Very often the sick person and his whole family suffer without being aware of this root cause of illness: the need for love.

Tom and his mother had always been very close. He had never married because of his mother's poor health. Whenever he displeased her, she would have heart flutters, so he tried to please her in every way he could.

We plainly see the mother's benefits. However, one day Tom's mother was found to have advanced cancer. The doctor told Tom that his mother had less than one year to live. Within three weeks, Tom became very ill and after a thorough examination, was told that he had leukemia. Tom's mother outlived him.

In this case, Tom also benefitted from his disease. The thought of living without his beloved mother was intolerable. He could not face the experience, so he subjectively chose to avoid it in the only way he knew. Other benefits may be less dramatic, but they also create the climate for illness.

When the bartering use of pain or illness is recognized by the sufferer, and recovery is more desired than the benefits received from suffering, a healing often follows. Such was the case of Lois. (All names are changed to protect the individual's privacy). Lois lived with her sister who was two years older than she. The sister, Jean, had always been an achiever and was an executive in a large firm. Lois had never had to face competition in the workaday world because she had a supportive husband. When her husband died, she moved in with her single sister, and soon afterwards began to experience pain in her back. She was relieved of any responsibility and given more attention than she had received since the death of her husband.

Jean began to suspect that Lois was settling back into a pattern of her childhood, a pattern that had once erased any need of competition between the sisters. Jean introduced Lois to the principles of her New Thought church. Lois entered classes in the church. Within six months, Lois began work in child care where the only requirements were those she excelled in—practical sense and loving care. Lois is no longer troubled with pain in her back.

George W. Meek, in *Healers and the Healing Process,* writes, "It does no good to say with the conscious mind, 'I want to be healed,' if deep in the subconscious there are thoughts and emotions that make illness more desirable than wholeness."

Benefits are a substitute for love. If you are suffering from a chronic physical condition, face the possibility that you are being rewarded with benefits which could be replaced with love. Love is available to you. It is found by first giving it. This realization may open up wonderful experiences for you. The more love you give to others, the more returns to you. In such an atmosphere, healing is found. It is a happy way to survive.

CHAPTER 4

The Need for Prayer, Insight, and Believing

Again I say unto you, that if two of you shall agree on earth as touching any thing that they shall ask, it shall be done for them of my Father which is in Heaven. For where two or three are gathered together in my name, there am I in the midst of them.

—Matthew 18: 19, 20

PRAYER PARTNERSHIP

YOU ARE NOT ALONE. If you want a healing, but your prayers appear to be cast on the wind, there is a way to receive that spiritual help you need. Often you pray for a healing, then continue to put more and more energy into the problem. You carry vivid pictures of the awfulness of the pain or disease. It is then you need a prayer partner —one who is not into the problem as you are.

If you can't get to a healing service or prayer workshop, send your request to a prayer ministry. Most churches have a prayer group, both New Thought churches and traditional churches. The most effective prayer is an affirmative one, as experience has shown. Since the universe does not deal in limitations, even the call, "God, help me!" has tremendous power. When the call is from a group consciousness, seeming miracles do happen. More than once I have called on the power of prayer groups. One changed my life in 1974.

For many years I had avoided religion of any kind. After a heart attack in 1973, I went to one specialist after another seeking some kind of help. My condition seemed to go from bad to worse. Asthma, a carry-over from childhood, became severe. I was found to have pulmonary fibrosis. I had a great fear of dying, though I often entertained the prospect of suicide. When my cardiologist scheduled the date for surgery, I fearfully pictured myself dying on the operating table. My old support systems, valium and vodka, were not providing the answer. Graced with a waiting period of five weeks before surgery was to take place, I had time to meditate and discover how much I desired to live.

There had to be a power greater than I to restore me. I couldn't do it alone, and no one else seemed able to do the job. I was single and no longer employable. In desperation, I called out to God, a mere acquaintance of mine. It was then I recalled a friend who attended a church where healings took place. What could I lose? I called Blanche and she took me to Founder's Church of Religious Science in Los Angeles the following Sunday.

In my tranquilized state, I remember only one thing the minister said, "There is a Power for good in the Universe greater than you are, and you can use it." Great! That took the responsibility from me (so I thought), but I discovered when I signed the prayer request form that I did have responsibility after all. There were instructions on how to pray affirmatively and how to change my belief about the problem. To my disappointment, however, there was no sympathy at all.

I had to give up my dependency on mind-altering chemicals to work this program right. After all, I did choose to live. I was given help by a group of people who were also trying to recover from the same dependency. I followed all the instructions given me by the prayer group and the recovery program offered by other recovering alcoholics.

After five weeks, I entered the hospital where I was given an angiogram and X-rays. The following morning my doctor came to my bed to give me an amazing report. My heart had proved to be a winner, and my X-rays showed that my lungs were in excellent condition. My doctor informed me that there was no reason I could not go back to work and live a fruitful life. That was a prescription I was ready to accept. It was then that I realized that I no longer coughed constantly; I breathed easily.

I continued to ask the affirmative prayer group for help because I had a life to straighten out, my own. I began to attend classes, to change my erroneous beliefs, and to change my life. Later, I entered the school of ministry, met the man I was to marry, and went on to become an ordained minister.

It is not necessary to carry your burdens alone. Reach for someone else, for prayer partnership.

In Chapter 7 you will find a format for a prayer workshop which anyone can use to form a support group for prayer partnerships.

HEALING INSIGHT

Webster's definition for "insight" is, "Sight or view of the interior of anything," "mental vision," "power to perceive readily and make clear and correct deductions."

Once we receive insight into the belief in sickness or pain, we can make clear and correct deductions and be on our way to a change of belief that makes healing possible.

STEPS TO CORRECT FAULTY DEDUCTIONS

1. Recognize that you alone cannot manage the situation.

2. Recognize that God, a Power greater than you, can restore you.

3. Make a conscious decision to turn your will and life over to the care of that Power.

4. Establish a purpose and number one priority to be healed.

5. Be willing to make the necessary changes.

6. Affirm and accept your wellness.

Healing insight is the mental search for a cause with intention of replacing it with a new cause that transforms a condition. Such an insight has led to the saving of many lives.

Gail Borden, over one hundred years ago, while crossing the Atlantic Ocean on board a ship, witnessed the death of two small children who had drunk contaminated milk. He became obsessed with a desire to find a way to preserve the freshness of milk. He tried and tried, failing many times. He kept trying, until, at last, he succeeded in discovering a method of producing condensed milk. Later, carved on Gail Borden's gravestone were these words, "I tried and failed. I tried again and again and succeeded."

Insight usually comes when we are willing to be open to a greater Intelligence, by going within and becoming listeners to direction.

SEE WHAT YOU BELIEVE

Everything you see is the result of your thoughts. There is no exception to this fact. Thoughts are not big or little, powerful or weak. They are merely true or false. Those that are true create their own likeness. Those that are false make theirs.

—From *A Course In Miracles*

The secret of visualization and the embodiment of an idea is, "see what you believe rather than believe what you see." The embodiment of your belief, especially the way you see yourself and the universe, has a direct relationship to your health. Your self-image is your self-fulfilling prophecy. The ability to change your self-image is within you and only needs to be motivated by your own energy.

William Randolph Hearst told this story about his experience of using mental imagery that produced a painful experience:

> Years ago I believed I had a bad heart. I was in a train headed for the Grand Canyon. The train stopped in the middle of the night. My heart began to pound. I called the porter and said, "Bring me a brandy. My heart can't stand the high altitude of the Grand Canyon." The porter said, "There ain't no brandy, no high altitude. We are in Needles, California and the sign says, '50 feet above sea level.'"

Jesus said, "Before they ask, I will answer." He healed by using the Principles of believing before seeing when he said to the lame man, "Pick up your bed and walk." To the man with the withered hand, Jesus said, "Stretch forth thine hand." To the dead man, he said, "Lazareth, come forth!" He spoke with the same foresight and insight that we are capable of using.

The scriptures tell us, "Decree a thing, and it shall be established unto thee." Decree it, believe it, and you too can be healed. What we persistently affirm, we increase; what we persistently deny, we decrease if we agree with our word.

For two years my mother was totally deaf. After testing her, the doctor informed me that she would never hear again, even with the aid of hearing devices. Nevertheless, her name remained on the prayer list in my church. On Mother's Day, the so-called 'impossible' happened. My husband and I visited her in the convalescent hospital. We began to communicate with pen and paper, as usual. Mother said, "That isn't necessary. I can hear you speaking!" She seemed as much surprised as we. Nurses now speak of this with awe. Mother's explanation of this was, "I didn't even pray to hear again. I just accepted it." Her acceptance was her way of seeing what she believed, rather than believing what 'appeared' to be true. Belief is the greatest mental coin.

CHAPTER 5

Affirmations to Heal

Every time you believe something, each time you declare something you believe, you set that law into motion which is the intelligence and vitality of body, mind and soul.

—From *Your Handbook for Healing,* by Craig Carter

THE MENTAL LAW we work with takes its impressions from our thoughts, inner images, feelings, and words. One of the first things a student of New Thought does is to learn to change his vocabulary, to remove from his conversation the negative words that are not appropriate for the new life he wishes to create. You will be healthier and less fearful when you remove such words as CAN'T, DON'T, SHOULD, SHOULDN'T, MUST, and MUSTN'T. These words can contribute to a poor self-image, give you "the guilts," and limit you.

Even worse than such an ill-star-studded vocabulary are the statements that serve as judge and jury to condemn your body, such as "I have heart trouble," "I have a bad back," "My poor feet!" and "I always get a cold . . ." Now, do you get the idea? The Creative Mind can only say yes to our words.

Many years ago, a French psychologist of the Nancy School made a discovery that we can change our lives with inspiring affirmations. Soon, thousands of people were affirming: "Every day in every way, I am getting better and better," as Emile Coué had suggested. And thousands found that it worked.

Your self-designed affirmations are more effective than those created for you by others. Beginners in the affirmative design of living may have difficulty creating their own affirmations. For that reason, I have included healing affirmations in this book.

For you who wish to design your own affirmations: first ask yourself what you really want to experience. Since 'being' is better than having, affirm yourself as being the person who is experiencing what you want to have. The less complicated the affirmation, the easier it is for you to affirm repeatedly. For example: "I see through perfect eyes" is more effective than "I have perfect eyes."

Avoid naming the problem, because naming it often turns it into an affirmation. You would not say, "I have a headache, and I am the person who doesn't have a headache." Rather, you would say, "My head is the perfect idea of God, and it is now whole." The Law you work with is very sensitive to the words you speak. The very mention of your problem tends to impress the Creative Law, which then responds accordingly.

When I was dependent on a wheelchair, walker, or cane, my constant affirmation was, "I walk with perfect ease, balance and rhythm."

Create your own affirmation, use it, and use it repeatedly. Your subjective mind will begin to accept your words into a belief system. Your words then become a reality. Remember the words of the Bible, "Be ye therefore transformed by the renewing of your mind."

THE POWER OF WRITTEN AFFIRMATIONS

Even more effective than spoken affirmations is the written word. It isn't easy to think or visualize your problems while you are affirming their opposite, but it is still harder to think negatively when you are writing your positive affirmation. The affirmations that are written are more firmly set in the Creative Mind. As you put forth the energy to think, then write and also see the words of your affirmation, that truth becomes set in the concrete of Creative Mind.

Joy, a friend who works with this technique and mails her affirmations to me, has an amazing success in manifesting them. Recently, she gave up her job and moved to Maryland. There, without a steady job (because she really prefers part-time employment), she decided that she wanted a two-story house, furnished with original art on the walls, sculptured objects, and lots of plants. I received the letter and treated for this to demonstrate for her, wishing at the same time that she had written a simpler affirmation.

Within two weeks, I got a phone call from Joy. She was ecstatic. A home owner, a Japanese gentleman who wanted to leave his home in the care of a reliable person for six months while he returned to his native country for a visit, had left Joy a two-story house, fully furnished with beautiful furniture, art, and sculpture. In and around the house was exotic plant life.

The same law that works so successfully for this woman will work for you if you do your part.

Write your affirmations.

AFFIRMATIONS THAT WORK

These affirmations are suggested to use as thought directives to change the patterns of your beliefs. Use your affirmation with regularity. It took time to establish faulty belief patterns, and it takes time to change them. Ask God's help to make this change, and time will be condensed for your corrected perception.

PERFECT HEALTH:
"I let Infinite Spirit within me—using whatever method It may—restore me to perfect health."

FEAR:
"I am filled with Love and Divine protection."

PAIN:
"I am free to experience comfort and wellness."

CONFUSION:
"Divine Wholeness obliterates every belief of confusion and discord from my life."

HEARING:
"My hearing is perfect. It is God in me hearing Its own voice."

MISTAKES:
"I am not bound by any mistakes, in my body or my affairs."

SKIN:
"My skin is the manifestation of Spirit in my body. It is perfect because it is Spirit."

SUPPLY:
"Universal Substance reflects Itself into my mind, into daily supply so that everything I need each day is supplied."

EYES:
"My eyes are the perfect eyes of God. My eyes are open and I see with clarity."

WEARINESS:
"I am renewed, alive, alert, and enthusiastic."

BELIEF IN INHERITED DISEASE:
"My Inner Light dissolves the belief of any tendency for inherited disease. I am free from the belief of bondage."

LEGS:
"I have two dependable, strong pillars to hold up my body temple. I bless them and see them as perfect."

CONGESTION:
"No congestion or false action is possible in my body. Perfect Life flows through me now. There is no fear, no congestion."

ENERGY:
Energy is Spirit's gift of Life to me. I use it wisely and well. Energy flows through me and I use it freely."

FALSE GROWTH:
"Every plant which my Heavenly Father hath not planted shall be uprooted and cast out."

BLOOD CIRCULATION:
"Life, as blood, flows in my body in perfect action, without obstruction, nourishing every part of my body perfectly."

BLOOD PRESSURE:
"Spirit knows only perfect blood pressure. I am at ease, releasing discord and anxiety. I experience excellent blood pressure."

BACK PAIN:
"My back is God's perfect idea in me. There is no burden or responsibility, no pressure to bear. I take my burdens to the Lord and leave them there."

FEET:
"I stand in God's Presence. My feet are at ease. They represent true understanding."

HANDS:
"Bless and use my hands, Father God, for the deeds You would have me do."

ARTHRITIS:
"The cells and bones in my body and all my affairs respond to a Peace that releases and heals."

FALSE HABITS:
"Every desire of my thought and heart is satisfied in the Truth. I am healed of the belief that there is true power in a false habit."

FEAR OF DEATH:
"There is no separation from God. Life evolves to a greater experience. I do not fear the unknown, for God is with me always."

HEART:
"My heartbeat and the rhythm of the Universe are one. Nothing can prevent its perfect action."

LUNGS:
"The lining of my lungs is renewed. Perfect action is established to conduct the breath of Life as if it were Spirit, because it *is* Spirit."

VOICE:
"Let the words of my mouth and the meditations of my heart be acceptable to Thee. Let my voice bring joy and love."

BONES:
"Everything that is needed to reveal perfection in the bones in my body is supplied, and I am made whole."

FEVER:
"Thank you, Loving Spirit, for fever which has now brought false effects to surface. Your Love is the Cause which now heals this body."

COLDS AND FLU:
"Confusion or discord are now identified, released, and cold / flu is no longer needed to flush out effect. I am made whole."

CANCER:
"Every confused or destructive cell in my body is brought into alignment with Intelligence and Harmony. God's Intelligence directs and corrects all cell action."

BREATH:
"Breath and Spirit are One. All organs and activity in my body honor this Spirit, I breathe with freedom and joy."

AFFIRMATION PRAYER KNOTS

Repetition of a statement will tend to create a reality to support the statement. How many realities have you created by a repetition of statements?

There is a game you can play with your mind and influence it to move from a sick old belief to a universal truth of perfection. You may call it your "affirmation prayer knots." After you have decided upon an affirmation of perfection, you may be ready to "string along" with this method, which is simple, like a game, and is at the same time very effective.

Cut a piece of string twenty-two inches long and tie twenty knots in the string at equal distances apart. Keep the string within reach at all times. You might keep it in your purse or pocket. Whenever you think of the problem which motivated the affirmation, take out your string and use it as a prayerful Catholic uses his prayer beads. This string is your "affirmation prayer knots" and it works on the same principle as prayer beads. You are mentally accepting the affirmation as truth with every knot. You are participating in your own healing.

One student, whose affirmation was, "I deserve to feel good all the time," used the prayer knots. Later, he said, "I am now reversing an old affirmation which was: 'I don't deserve to be well.' Until now, I wasn't aware of what was going on in my head."

Another method you may use with your finger tips may add a little "snap" to your life. This is a "tough love" method. Keep a rubber band on your wrist during a period when you find yourself worrying about a physical condition. Each time you discover fearful thoughts going through your mind, snap the rubber band. This is the same principle as aversion therapy which is very successful in the cure of smoking and other harmful habits.

These methods for changing habits of thought are indeed primitive, but consider this, your subjective mind is also primitive. It does not operate from reason or logic but acts from your conscious and even unconscious direction.

Do these exercises in the spirit of fun.

CHAPTER 6

Visualization and Relaxation for Healing

Always visualize the effect you want, not the process. The demonstration is what you want. Leave the mechanics to the Law of Mind.

MENTAL EMBODIMENT

A DEMONSTRATION OR HEALING is created from a mental concept where the mental equivalent of the desire is nurtured until it matures into effect. The mind fashions a model of the belief and embodies it by mental vision. For example, if you picture yourself as one who gets a cold whenever you sit in a draft, Creative Mind will act to produce the cold from that belief. Embodiment of a wholesome body now, beginning with visualization of yourself as a healthy and vibrant person, can bring about your healing.

Embodiment is a belief exercise. How does one know the difference between wishing or hoping and visualization and embodiment? There is a mental energy required in visualization. You actually play the role in mind that you want to manifest.

For example: You have an appointment with your doctor. Many tests have been made, and there is a possibility that when he reads the reports today there will be some very bad news. How can you visualize in such a way as to leave a mental imprint of "very good results" on the Creative Mind and thus avoid problems? Simple: Visualize yourself walking out of the doctor's office with a happy prayer of gratitude because of the good news.

Visualization is now being taught in medical clinics that treat cancer, in pain clinics, and as a method for bio-feedback as well as in other types of therapy. It is the use of Power of the Mind. You can use it to heal yourself. It is your Divine gift.

A woman came into my office suffering with severe pain caused by a large lump in her side. Her doctor had advised surgery, but she feared surgery and believed it could be avoided. Although I suggested that she continue seeing her physician, we began with Spiritual Mind Treatment, and I suggested she meditate at least three times a day and visualize the lump in her side as a large ball of Jello being dissolved by the heat of her body. I told her that she was in charge of the heat, and all she had to do was to feel the heat in her side and visualize the Jello dissolving.

Five days later, after following my suggestion, she went back to her doctor. He could not locate the lump. All pain was gone.

During my recovery from surgery following my accident, my doctor was in doubt that I would ever be able to bend my right knee. Each day, several times, I visualized bending my knee to a greater degree than before. Each day I was able to bend my knee to a greater degree, and within three months I was able to bend my knee normally.

RELAXATION

Dr. Edward Taub and his wife Barbara, who is a registered nurse, use the White Light concept as an aid in healing in their clinic in California. The Alpha state induced provides the mental climate for healing. Although you may use the instructions given when you are alone, it will no doubt be more effective if someone else guides you into the relaxation exercise and the White Light.

Relaxation Exercise

Find a quiet place where there will be no interruptions and sit comfortably with nothing on your lap or in your hands. Close your eyes. Be aware that your body is servant to your mind and is prepared to obey its instructions. Give your body these suggestions, or they may be given by a participant. The instructions are as follows:

Allow all your muscles to tighten, stressing muscles throughout your entire body. Remain with muscles tightened for a few seconds. Now, relax all your muscles. Relax the muscles in your feet, your toes, insteps, and heels. Now relax the calves of your legs . . . relax your thighs . . . relax your hips and your buttocks . . . relax your belly . . . relax your waist, all around. Be aware of the muscles in your back as you relax them, up from the waist. Let the muscles go limp. The muscles in the rib cage are relaxing, and now across the shoulders, the muscles are relaxing. Feel the muscles relax in the stomach . . . across the chest . . . all the muscles in the breast relax and also under the arms. Now, relax the muscles in the upper arms, relax . . . relax the lower arms and wrists . . . relax the palms of your hands and fingers and thumbs.

The hands are loose and relaxed. Feel the muscles in your neck and jaws relax . . . relax the muscles around your lips and nostrils. Relax the cheeks and around the eyes. Let the eyes go soft . . . now the muscles in your temples are relaxing. Relax the brows and forehead. Now, you are at peace. You are relaxing all the muscles in your body.

Imagine being ready to step into an elevator. You are on the 10th floor. You mentally step into the elevator. You push the button to descend. As you watch the numbers above the door of the elevator you see that as you are now passing the 9th floor, the number lights up. As you pass each floor, its number is indicated by the light behind it. As you descend, you will also be descending into the Alpha state, deeper and deeper. Now, you are descending to the 8th floor. Watch the light above the door. You are now on the 8th floor. You are relaxing more with each floor. Now, you are passing the 7th floor. Relax. You are descending to the 6th floor. Now the 5th floor. As you watch the light above the door move to a lower number, you relax more. Now you are on the 4th floor. Relax. You are passing the 3rd floor . . . the 2nd floor. You are descending to the 1st floor, and you are relaxing in every part of your body.

You have just descended to the Alpha state of receptivity. When you are ready to return from the Alpha state you will be instructed to mentally ascend in the same manner.

THE WHITE LIGHT

White Light is now entering your toes and moving up into your feet. Now it moves up your ankles and into the calves of your legs and into your thighs. The White Light moves up through the passages to the bladder, filling the bladder with light. Now the light fills the kidneys with healing radiance. The White Light's healing glow is in the intestines . . . stomach is filled with light . . . White Light moves into the heart, regulating the heartbeat . . . the light now fills the lungs, repairing the tissue and removing obstructions . . . the light shines in the esophagus, in the throat and head. The White Light moves around the eyeballs, renewing the tissue and begins the dissolving action to remove any threatening obstructions . . . the light fills the ears and inner ears . . . now the light moves throughout the sinuses and brain, renewing as it goes. White Light fills the arms and hands. You feel its presence in your fingertips. The light now fills every vein and artery of your body, regulating pressure and purifying the cells of the blood. It moves into the nervous system. The body is filled with White Light.

Experience the White Light in your body as peace and wellness. Now let that light move out beyond your body, healing your affairs as it touches your total atmosphere. See the light move out from you, surrounding you and out, out into the universe. Take your time to picture and feel this.

You will now remain in this relaxed state as we ascend again to the tenth floor and out of the Alpha state. You are again in the elevator of your mind going up. Watch the lighted indicator. There, see the floors flash as we ascend . . . Picture the 2nd floor indicated . . . now the 3rd floor . . . you pass the 4th floor . . . there is the 5th floor . . . the 6th floor . . . see the 7th floor being lighted on the indicator . . . there is the 8th floor . . . now the 9th floor. Even with the increased awareness of the circumstances around you, you remain in a relaxed state. Now you are on the 10th floor. The door of the elevator opens, and you mentally step out.

The White Light has been used successfully in training the subjective mind to be aware of the healing process taking place in the body.

Use this method regularly. You will benefit from the relaxation of the meditative state while you will be methodically healing your body.

CHAPTER 7

Making Healing Happen

For what is time without a past and future? It has taken time to misguide you so completely, but it takes no time at all to be what you are . . . nothing can reach you here out of the past, and it is here that you are completely free and wholly without condemnation.

—From *A Course In Miracles*

HEALING'S RELATIONSHIP TO TIME

A MYSTIC KNOWS that in the exalted moment of illumination, the conception of time is nonexistent. Time is not God's creation, but that of man. We created this limiting experience to witness the moving from one learning phase to another.

Time is measured by memory. When we can learn from every memory and move forward in our spiritual growth because of these lessons, we will find that time has been beneficial. We will understand our need for time.

Each day, we search our memory for perception to form a model for our experiences. All conditions, failures, and pain that existed yesterday are patterns from memory out of which we cut the cloth of today's fabric. And, so, servants of time are made, enslaved by memory.

Some of the evidence of memory servitude can be seen in people who are accident prone, failure programmed, quickly aging, and those who are chronically ill. Corrected perception is necessary for these people to be healed. This is possible only when the need for change is greater than the comfort of a familiar memory pattern.

TRANSCENDING TIME

The consciousness in a mystical experience is one which transcends time. The moment of illumination contains no memory, no dimensions, no past or future. The experiences of the mystics that have been reported have witnessed being One with the Universe in a moment when time seemed to stop. It is my opinion that many of us who seek the Presence of God, desiring It above all else, have experienced this timeless moment.

The booklet "The Golden Key," by Emmet Fox, offers a practical exercise that anyone can use to correct memory and practice the Presence and, in doing so, manifest a healing. In the booklet, Emmet Fox tells you to stop thinking about the difficulty, whatever it is, and think about God instead. The booklet has only six pages, but it explains in the simplest way how to practice this healing art of correcting time's memory. This experience is like touching the hem of the mystical garment.

"Spiritual Treatment" is an affirmative prayer with the mental discipline of releasing memory and mentally transcending time, seeing only the gift as already given. A practitioner is trained to do this by the education of his or her perception. By applying the principles in this book you, too, can transcend time, experience the Presence of God, and be a channel for your own healing or the healing of others. Such a one is called a Miracle Worker in *A Course in Miracles.*

GIVE THANKS AND SHARE YOUR HEALING

Giving thanks should not be held in escrow until your healing manifests. You are worthy of wellness, and there is a Power that can and will heal you if given permission. Your doubt is a refusal of permission.

Examine your feelings carefully. If doubt arises in your mind, look at the roots of that doubt. You will probably discover why you have found it necessary to suffer. Have you been believing in a vengeful deity? Do you not know that God is Love, and Love sees no error? There is no judgment where Love is. Do you not know that you were made in the image and likeness of Love and were created by It? There can be no Divine reason for denying you the healing you desire.

You do not give thanks for what you are not to receive. You only give thanks for what you do receive. Here is where faith is of great importance. When we ask with true believing, we are to give thanks at that time. The subjective mind we work with is very impressionable; and when we constantly give thanks upon requesting our good, that mind responds by accepting our good as already designed, then manifests it.

Often, we pray for wellness; then when we begin to experience it, the doubting mind says, "yes, but . . ." How can such a healing be permanent?

Ask for your wellness, believing. Pay the coin of gratitude by giving thanks upon request, and this will manifest the good you ask. It is that simple. The difficult part is changing the old idea that a thing is not given until you experience it in your senses or feelings. Giving thanks will help you change from the old idea and strengthen your faith.

When you experience your healing, share it with others. You would not refrain from giving water to a thirsty person. When you share your healing with another, you are giving him a reason to believe and be healed.

The good news of healing was shared by Phineas P. Quimby, the father of New Thought; by Charles and Myrtle Fillmore, who founded Unity; and Nona Brooks who, with Malinda Cramer, founded Divine Science. All had experienced a miraculous healing and in sharing their good news caused thousands to believe and be healed. Your own healing can be so shared. Your healing can be your gift to others.

Margaret Cousins, the Canadian figure-skating champion, at the peak of her career became paralyzed and was confined to a wheel chair with no hope of walking again. She became depressed and felt that there was no chance. Although she was not of the Catholic faith, she was encouraged by a friend to visit Brother Andre's Shrine where many went to be healed.

Margaret's automobile was equipped with hand controls so that she could drive. With her wheel chair placed beside her, she drove to the shrine of the Catholic priest, Brother Andre. She found it to be in a building with many steps and a steep ramp. She pulled herself up the ramp, painfully, and into the building.

Margaret found the large room where the heart of the priest was suspended in a bottle of liquid. The bottle was on a pedestal. Margaret Cousins was fascinated with the exhibited heart and drew herself up closely to better view the heart. It was then that she realized that she was actually standing on her feet. She stood there astonished, took a small step forward, then called out, "Where do I go to report a healing?"

When you have been healed, report your healing. What you declare as yours becomes your keepsake.

HEALING PERCEPTION WORKSHOP

To correct perception, you change destructive belief patterns to Truth and wholeness. This is done in the same manner used in learning a new language, with repetition and familiarity. If you wish to learn French, you learn to think in that language, and you share with others in that language. This is how you learn a new language. To heal perception, you learn to think in a new way and you share with others in the same way. In an intensive workshop with others who wish to learn and establish a new belief in their own Divinity and wholeness, you accelerate the process of correcting and healing your perception.

With conscious intent and effort you remove the buildup of belief packed into your subjective mind by race-consciousness, misconceptions, and directions of old faulty thought patterns. Have you ever tried to remove, by a solvent only, a build-up of paint on an old piece of furniture? Time and work are required to remove the paint so that you can start with a new look. This principle governs corrected perception. Remove old ideas and replace them with new ones.

Here are some ideas to use to form your own support group and learn a new way of life. Prepare in advance by requiring that only those people participate who sincerely wish to be healed and are willing to commit themselves to whatever is necessary for changing faulty perceptions about their bodies. A commitment to attendance and homework, and to taking the responsibility for their lives and experiences, is necessary to be a part of this self-healing and life-changing group. Of course, confidentiality is a requirement.

You may start with as few as four people, but no more than twelve. Write each name on a slip of paper for the 'prayer Partner' drawing and arrange the chairs in a circle before each meeting. There should be a weekly workshop with regularity, no more than one or two hours, determined by the number of participants.

BODY AND MIND TRANSFORMATION WORKSHOP

1. Opening prayer (rotate with different participant weekly.)

2. Each person writes an affirmation for healing on a piece of paper. The facilitator takes them and each person draws a slip from the affirmation bowl. This is their activity, to use the affirmation for the week to come.

3. Each week the participants draw names from the slips the facilitator has prepared. The facilitator explains the importance of praying for the healing of the person whose name is drawn.

4. There is a two-minute meditation in silence. The facilitator then reminds the group to practice meditation daily, to improve their conscious contact with God.

5. In round-robin fashion, each participant repeats these three steps:

   A. I recognize that my own thoughts and beliefs have created painful experiences in my life.

   B. I believe that there is a Power Greater than I am Who can restore me to wholeness.

   C. I now turn my will and my life over to the care of God and become willing to change my belief at depth.

6. Facilitator explains the importance of writing your goals and affirmations. This is the way we impress ideas on our subjective mind.

7. Sharing Time. No one is compelled to speak if he wishes not to. Here are guidelines for those who participate: honesty, confidentiality, responsibility, no judgment or interrupting the speaker. The facilitator may tap the table to remind the speaker if he has exceeded the time limit, or when he is playing a PLOM (Poor Little Old Me) tape.

   Suggested topics for discussion: Spiritual breakthroughs, belief-changing experiences, personal disciplines for healing and Spiritual growth, letting go and letting God, and demonstrations of answered prayer. (You may add to this list from group suggestions.)

8. (Optional) Discuss visualization and its method and values. There are many good books on Creative Visualization to be recommended.

9. Closing prayer (again, rotate).

CHAPTER 8

The Healing Place

THE "SPIRITUAL COIN" is the awareness and embodiment in your Higher Power. It is the coin of belief. You pay the coin when you lay down all the burdens of life, become quiet, and go within. You embody the nature of God when you experience the Oneness with God and all creation. For this coin you will find your Healing Place.

You want to find a place to be healed. There is a place where you can go when you are lonely, sick, in need, hurt, or afraid. It is your very own sanctuary. In this place you find love, perfection, peace, and protection. You can go there any time. Each time you enter this place, you grow stronger, less afraid, less lonely, and happier is a way you've never known. You find that you are never alone there. The Comforter is there. This is your Healing Place. Remember, your spiritual coin is awareness, embodiment of the perfect nature of God, and a belief in Its Healing Power.

The way to your Healing Place is to go empty handed. You cannot take your problems with you. No burdens may enter this precious place. Even mental activity, your life-time practice, is not welcome and may not enter.

In your Healing Place you will find that circumstances and conditions you have accepted as reality are not your true reality at all. You are a part of a greater reality that makes your healing possible. This greater reality is God's Perfection, and Its reflection in you results in your healing. As you begin to observe the True Reality which is Perfect God, Perfect Being, your body begins to align with the Truth that all is God, and the healing begins. If you understood this Truth now, there would be no need to be healed. But you do not understand Perfection now. You do understand a need to know the way of healing.

Ernest Holmes said, "We enter the Absolute to the degree that we withdraw from the relative." The energy you put into any thought that is not on the Absolute is drawing you into the relative to a greater degree. You cannot always be in the Heaven of Spirit. There is no account of anyone who could live that way. Even Jesus loved parties, but he was close enough to that "heaven" that he was able to see the Christ in everyone. It is this state of awareness that you strive to have.

It is obvious that any healing, to be permanent, must first begin within thought. Thought then affects and conducts energy.

We certainly do not argue with any method of healing that works. We do recognize that every person healed, whether by means of medical science, yoga, or voodoo, has a common reason that makes it possible. That is belief. As Jesus said to the one whom he healed, "Thy faith hath made thee whole." But belief in the method does not keep you well. Belief in the Healer within and the mental action of healed thoughts can make a healing permanent.

The question is, how do we get healed thoughts? Jesus said, "Seek ye first the Kingdom of God and His Righteousness, and all these things shall be added unto you." He spoke also of the Kingdom of Heaven, and declared it is within. If the Kingdom of God and the Kingdom of Heaven are One; then the Divinity is within you and available as are "all things." Then, isn't this the Healing Place?

You want to be healed. It may be a mental condition where fear, deep anger, guilt, or feelings of loss dominate. It may be sickness, pain, or disease that threatens. It may be a financial problem that needs to be healed. All the thoughts that accompany the problem are thoughts that need to be healed. You seek the answer. If seeking the Righteousness mentioned in the promise can bring about the answer you want, how, then, is it done? You can do it! You may not be a religious person. You may have made many mistakes and may be making them now; yet this transformation is possible for you too.

As early conscious man contemplated his life, he realized that a Power greater than himself was necessary and did exist. Even as today, the Power early man recognized could not be understood. Man could not comprehend the unlimited nature of God, so he created God as an idol, as elements of nature, and then he made the worst of all mistakes: man created Him in his own image.

We have not departed far from that idea of an anthropomorphic God; yet Jesus said that God was not to be found "lo here nor lo there." His message was: "God is Spirit, and they that worship Him must worship Him in Spirit and in truth." Even as he spoke this, Jesus must have known that it was necessary to identify God by masculine gender in order to lend credibility to the statement.

Man has always longed for a Higher Power. There is a deep yearning in you for God, as with every person. You may never understand this great instinctive drive within you that might be compared to the need of a flower to turn to face the sun. No matter which way you turn the flower pot, the plant will find a way to face the light. The eternal spirit within you will find a way to seek and find the Light.

That Light is your Comforter. When Jesus referred to the Holy Spirit as Comforter, he was calling upon an attribute of God that has always been available but seldom recognized. Until you recognize this part of the Divine Nature, you limit your comforting use of It. This Nature is pure Spirit. The line of communication is through your own spirit.

There is no familiar, beloved figure or symbol to lead you to the God you seek. You have been told to turn within. As often as you have heard these words, you are sometimes uncertain of their meaning. Does it mean to be still, to talk to God, or simply to listen, hoping a message will come? It can mean any of these.

To bridge the chasm between old ideas of a masculine, man-made God and the One Universe that is God, go within, using a mental equivalent of a place of peace. See it as your peaceful haven, a refuge in troubled times, your home where you seek God and experience your own "Healing Place."

This habit of going within has its effect as a greater sense of awareness, an ability to see people and circumstances as less threatening. There is more peace and less fear in your life. As a result, your body is affected by this transformation. The network of Intelligence throughout your body gets the message of peace and responds to it.

If your pain or problem is in some area of your body, go there mentally. Try to see the place as it appears within. Impossible? No, not at all! There is an Intelligence within you that you can use. You do not really have to know what that Healing Place looks like, but you can create its reality. Visualize it as a chapel or some other peaceful place.

At first, it may take time to arrive at the state of meditation, to let go of all thoughts and just picture that location and be in it. If you think you cannot visualize, here is a suggestion: take a moment and think of your home or apartment or perhaps the house you lived in as a child. Count the doors in it. If you can do this, you can visualize. Now turn within and let the greater Intelligence reveal your Healing Place.

When you mentally see your Healing Place and experience being there, cease thinking with your logical mind and just feel yourself within this area. Do not think of pain or discord in the area, but be there and meditate on God, which is the Kingdom. God, being omnipresent, is right there.

When wayward thoughts present themselves, such as, "This doesn't make sense," or "How can this heal my thoughts and body?"—just let the thoughts go. Logic is an ego creation. To recognize God and acknowledge your Oneness, is seeking the Kingdom and Its Righteousness. In this Inner place is your healing.

You will find after practicing this that your thoughts take on a new peace, and fears subside. Something is happening! First, your thoughts are healed. There is a shift in consciousness as you begin to let go beliefs about the problem. You find God where the problem was. Don't be discouraged if for a while the pain still announces itself. The power of the pain or problem cannot long compete with the Power you are now experiencing. You are working in the field of Righteousness.

If your problem is one of relationships, loss, or lack, go within and have the feeling of physically and totally being there. Still using your mental sight, see yourself in a chapel or place where you feel God's presence and think on the loving attributes of God. Let go all thoughts of the problem. You will find that the ego holds on to them, holds on to hurts, retaliation, and fear. Remember, such are ego's defenses and they have served to create the problem. Simply unplug ego's energy by thinking on God.

It is important to be consistent. This is the secret of your success in healing. You are now creating a holy place where you can go to find peace. With regular practice, you find life around you changing, you find more love, and you find peace where discord once lived. Your blood-pressure comes into balance, your breathing is easier, your sleeping problems go.

These are only a few of the benefits that come with the healing of your thoughts about discord. Remember, you have spent many years programming your subjective mind with belief in discord and separation. The new program of recognizing God where the problem is found, must be practiced over and over. You may go into this Kingdom whenever and wherever you like. There is no one to know but you. It is your place of peace, but you cannot take your problem there.

You have suffered pain and discord and belief in separation because you have not been given the road map to your Divine destiny. You have traveled over painful terrain and do not understand, but there is a Comforter awaiting you. You have been told to ask and it shall be given, seek and you shall find, knock and it shall be opened unto you. It is time for you to ask, seek, and knock at the door of the Kingdom. You will begin to see evidence of your Divine destiny, the gift in your problem. Enter the Kingdom, your Healing Place, your refuge in time of trouble.

Since man discovered God within, he has found the way to enter the Kingdom. Scientists today are discovering that prayer and meditation bring about an altered state of consciousness called the "Alpha State." This remarkable discovery has not changed meditation or prayer, but it does reveal to the skeptics that something is happening to one who enters the Kingdom. Ernest Holmes stated, "We believe that the Kingdom of Heaven is within and that we experience this Kingdom to the degree that we become conscious of It."

If the problem appears to be another person, enter the Kingdom and from that viewpoint, see the Glory of God embracing you and the other person. This is the Divine Light that heals you both. Visualize a golden light surrounding you and the other person. Do this often and "all things shall be added unto you." In that light of peace, forgiveness, love, and a release of fear, you will be healed. Even the other person will appear to change.

The Healing Place is a state of being. You go within and just *be.* It is as simple as that. You may recognize the nature of God in such things as peace, love, forgiveness, givingness, and any other attribute you can think of. If you have any difficulty in arriving at this quiet state of meditation, just remind yourself of these qualities. Do not think of the problem. Think about God; be in the Kingdom.

You are not dictating to God in this receptive state, and the Light of God shines through all the problems and reveals your Divinity in your moment of Oneness. Oneness is your natural state; experience it often by entering the Kingdom. Your Healing Place and the Kingdom are One. It is so simple. Just enter the Healing Place and recognize the Presence there. It is your very own, and in It you can be healed.

When suddenly a problem arises, you need not panic, for now you know there is a place where you can go for help. It is a place where no problem can enter. It is a place where you can experience God and be healed. It is the Kingdom of God, and it is right within you. You pay the spiritual coin of belief in Its Healing Power and enter. It is your own Healing Place.